Jazz Superheroe

Billie Holiday

Lady Day

by Eve Zanni

A note from the author

Jazz speaks for life -- Dr. Martin Luther King, Jr.

What's your story? -- Lester Young *Prez*

No two people on earth are alike and it's got to be that way in music or else it isn't music.
– Billie Holiday *Lady Day*

The Jazz Superheroes' *his-tories* and *her-stories* are America's story told in music. Music is riffing off a story…Stories bear witness to what was, what is, what will be. Stories bring present the ancestors, predecessors and the soul stirrers: the creators of music who wove words, gave voice, danced up rhythms…

Music is the message of the people and is essentially connected to spiritual, emotional, social, and political movement. And music will carry our stories to those who will come after us.

The Jazz Superheroes were those *giants who walked the earth* that I used to hear my parents and their friends talk about. I grew up in a home full of music and musicians and stories. When the elders spoke about their jazz heroes I thrilled to the sound of wonder I heard in their voices…I knew that these were stories I wouldn't hear in school. These folks had seen, heard or played with some of these giants. They were witnesses.

I am a singer, educator of jazz vocal and instrumental music and composer of music and lyrics. When I sing one of the great jazz standards, a historic blues, or any heartfelt music, I feel connected to all music and musicians. I feel that we all share a common *spiritage* through the *river of life current* that feeds the continuation of life's story.

My passion for **The Jazz Superheroes** comes from *The Blues* that the enslaved Africans shared so they could survive in a strange new land. From African heritage, they created an American *spiritage;* the gift of true feeling carried through the veins of music that flows to all hearts that listen. This is the truth that **The Jazz Superheroes** knew. The music they made will live long after we are gone. Everyone has a story. Yours is completely unique. We are all sounds in Life's symphony.

What's your story?   Pass it on…

Eve Zanni, New York City, October 9, 2017

How to use The Jazz Superheroes Books

Tell the story

Everyone loves a good story. Tell the stories of American Jazz heroes because they are America's story. Tell them in your own voice and speak the words aloud to others; younger people, older people, babies. Tell these stories because they come to life when we see them in our minds, feel them in our hearts and hear them in our thirsty ears.

Share the story

To be gifted with the telling of a story is a life-changing experience. Share these stories in homes, classrooms, churches, synagogues, mosques, parks. Let's build a culture that shares the lessons of our music heroes before those lessons are forgotten. As a longtime music educator, teacher of vocal and instrumental jazz, I discovered the secret ingredient to teaching jazz: the stories behind the music! Every note of jazz, blues and world music is a story.

Listening examples

Each book has selected listening examples that deepen the experience of the stories, to be played at the indicated parts of the story. Take the time to listen, as you pause, in the story. All the links are free from YouTube, Spotify or Deezer. Song downloads can be purchased from ITunes for a nominal fee, or you can use something similar from your own collection.

Hidden History

The essence of jazz was born in Africa, stolen, thrown into ships, survived unimaginable suffering. The songs, wails, shouts and beats of the kidnapped Africans carried longing for their Mother Land, loved ones, their language; the life they knew. This deep longing was the sound that became *The Blues*. Everyone has felt longing and everyone has had *The Blues*. *The Blues* essence gave birth to Jazz, Broadway, Rhythm n' Blues, Reggae, Heavy Metal, Hip Hop, Rock n' Roll, Country, all forms of American popular music. *The Blues* lives in the heart of American music. It has become the music of a vast new World and America's proudest voice.

A lot of true events never made it to the history books in America. People will be surprised to hear some of the stories in this book series, or shocked that they are being told. But as Superhero Charlie Parker said, *"Now is the Time"*.

Super Hero Billie Holiday "Lady Day "

Twinkle Lady: a torch song for hip grownups and soulful kids (to the tune of Twinkle Twinkle Little Star)

Lady Day, she paid some dues, her whole life was like the blues

So much feeling in her song; sassy, classy, sweet and strong,

Lady Day she paid some dues, her whole life was like the blues

Super Statistics

Name: (Eleanora Fagan) Billie Holiday

Nickname: *Lady Day* or *Lady*

Born: April 7, 1915 in Philadelphia, Pennsylvania

Died: July 22, 1959 in New York City

Intro

Billie Holiday changed jazz singing permanently and forever. She influenced all the singers and musicians, such as Peggy Lee, Carmen McRae, Anita O'Day, Frank Sinatra, Diana Ross, Madeline Peyroux, Abbey Lincoln, Andra Day; even Bob Dylan was inspired by Lady Day. And what we all learn from her makes our own music richer. But no one sounds like her.

She is famous for the sadness and loneliness carried in her voice. Most people who hear her for the first time are struck by the deep feelings that her voice expresses. And maybe a little scared by what they are feeling, too....she could hypnotize and move an audience to feel strong emotions when she sang a song that told a sad truth, such as *Strange Fruit.* My own parents heard her perform it and were moved to tears. When she sang a *torch song* about lost love, people thought of their own lost loves and felt her pain. She was an artist who painted strong pictures, but instead of paint and canvas, she used her voice to create strong emotions in her listeners. Billie said "Without feeling, whatever you do amounts to nothing". You can hear her super emotional singing powers when you listen to her on CD or see her on YouTube.

When she sang happy and sassy songs, you can hear her voice playing rhythmically with the notes. She could also *color* and *shade* the tones of her voice. There is a playful bounce in her voice that all the musicians playing with her seemed to catch. No other singer ever sounded as much a part of the band as Billie did. It's as though her voice was another instrument in the group.

Super Powers

Singing Powers: She sounded something like a horn, as her voice slipped and slid around the melody, bending the notes. She sang like she was one of the instruments in the group, yet each word was crystal clear. Sometimes she sang behind the beat, which gave her a lazy, relaxed, takin'-my-time-if-you-please-attitude. Her voice could bounce and tease. Her sassy, rebellious side pops out in some songs, like *T'ain't Nobody's Business if I Do*. That's when you know that she had a hard life and could be tough. You wouldn't have wanted to mess with her when she was in that mood. When Lady sang a love song she could make you see the pearly shine of a full moon: her phrases graceful and elegant…. She could also croon and coo, like a mother bird, tender and intimate with her baby.

Super Beauty: Billie Holiday was beautiful. She stood tall and stately; she had light coffee-with-milk-colored skin, and masses of soft gently-curling dark hair. She usually wore her signature white gardenias in her hair. Her singing career would have sailed along just fine, with her beauty and wonderful singing style, but she was not satisfied just singing the popular songs of the day. Those songs made people happy and contented and described a world that was fine for everyone. But things were not fine for everyone and Billie wanted to tell the truth.

Super Courage: Billie had deep feelings of hurt, anger and outrage, at the way her people, the African American people of color, were treated. She was extremely courageous and decided to sing a heart-rending song about the ravages of murderous racism. This took guts because she might have lost a lot of singing engagements, and probably did. She could have lost some of the fans that bought her recordings because they didn't want to hear any serious music, just the fun stuff. But her feelings were strong, and she went ahead and took a chance on losing some of her popularity by singing the ballad *Strange Fruit*. The year was 1939. Hitler's campaign of *Racism* and *Anti-Semitism* was on the rise in Europe and *The Civil Rights Movement* was still a good 20 years in the future.

Super Song Writing: Billie Holiday wrote some very important and memorable songs. She wrote the lyrics to *God Bless the Child* in 1939, and Arthur Herzog wrote the music. It became one of her big hits. Thousands of singers and musicians have recorded it and many people still sing it today. She also wrote some other very important songs that have been recorded by many artists and are still sung today. She wrote *Fine and Mellow, Billie's Blues, Don't Explain, Lady Sings the Blues* and more.

Super Survivor Spirit: The story of Billie Holiday's life, in her own words, was like a story from a tragic novel. She had the spirit of a super hero to be able to carry on and continue to give her incredible music to the world during her very short life of only 44 years. The violence and horror that she experienced as a young person would have destroyed or disabled most people. She thought that the alcohol she drank and the drugs she used would ease her pain and make the horrible facts of life for a woman artist of color hurt a little less. But these substances ruined her health instead. Nowadays people are more informed about the bad effects of these substances but in those days most people didn't know. Even doctors thought that cigarettes were good for your health! Billie was dedicated to telling the truth in her music; even the hard facts of life for African Americans. Most people know more about Billie's substance addiction and her mistakes than about her music and her activism. And history proves that her music, her survivor spirit, and dedication to sharing her deepest feelings through her voice as a force for good, make her a Super Hero.

Lady and the Writers

Super History

Very few people have had such a sad, hard life as Billie Holiday and lived to tell about it. In spite of everything that tried to beat her down, she became one of the most beloved singers in the history of the human race.

Billie was born to two very young parents. Her mom, Sadie and her dad, Clarence, were both teenagers on April 7, 1915, when Billie was born in Philadelphia, Pennsylvania. Billie's given name was Eleanora Fagan. Sadie did housework and washed clothes to make a living. Clarence was a musician who played banjo and guitar. He played with some of the best bands of the time, including the great Fletcher Henderson. Clarence moved around a lot, between Baltimore, Philadelphia and New York, chasing the music and women, too.

Alone Together

Eleanora's mom, Sadie never had much luck. It seems that her parents and their families didn't really care much about her. But she was a neat and clean, hard working young woman. It was bitterly hard for a teenage girl of color with a baby to earn a living in those days. No one helped out much. Sadie often had to leave Eleanora with people she knew while she took jobs out of town to make a few dollars. Some of these people were not very kind to Eleanora who must have missed her mom a lot.

Sadie learned how to sew beautiful clothes for Eleanora. When Sadie cleaned houses for rich white people, they sometimes gave her their children's used clothes, which she brought home for her daughter. Billie remembered that when she was little Eleanora, growing up in the slums of Baltimore, she was always dressed beautifully and was the *sharpest kid on the block.*

Sad Little Eleanora

First Nightmares

Little Eleanora had many horrifying experiences while she was growing up. When she was very young, she visited her great-grandmother. They lay down together and after telling Eleanora a story, they both fell asleep. When Eleanora woke up, her great-grandmother's arms were locked around the little girl's neck, but she was dead. Poor Eleanora was so freaked out, she screamed and yelled until someone came in to help release her. She had constant nightmares for many years after that and was afraid to fall asleep.

But being awake was sometimes a nightmare for Eleanora as well. She noticed that black people and white people lived by different sets of rules and in very different conditions.

Unfair!

Baltimore had lots of beautiful houses where rich white folks lived. Long flights of wide, white steps led up to the front doors. Eleanora could get 15 cents for scrubbing these steps on her hands and knees. The work was hard and scraped her fingers. She knew that there had to be a better way to get money.

The streets of West Baltimore were rough, rowdy and run-down. Most of the people who lived there were very poor. Things were hard for Sadie and Eleanora. There was never enough work, and Sadie still worked at jobs that took her away from Eleanora for days at a time.

Sometimes Eleanora's father, Clarence stopped by to visit which Eleanora loved. He was a musician and always dressed real sharp. The only other people who dressed nice and seemed to have a few dollars in their pockets were the men and women who hung out on the streets and did illegal things. Eleanora probably looked up to them a little, because her own mom, with all her hard, honest work, never seemed to get much.

Eleanora saved up her pennies to go to the movies. There, she discovered the glamorous and beautiful movie star Billie Dove. Billie Dove's nickname was *The American Beauty*. She wore gorgeous gowns, furs and jewels. Many of her film characters were strong and independent women. This was very unusual in the 1920's. Women in films were usually just pretty and weren't supposed to be smart or strong. Eleanora admired Billie Dove a lot. Maybe she was inspired by her elegance, strength and independence. She must have seemed so different from Eleanora's poor mom, Sadie and from most of the people in her neighborhood. Billie Dove wasn't rubbing her hands red and ragged, scrubbing white peoples' clothes or steps. Eleanora loved how her name sounded, and began calling herself *Billie*. With Sadie gone so often, Billie learned to make her own way around. She learned to be tough, to protect herself from the rough people on the streets. Billie hated school and began to play hooky. She hated being bossed around by anybody, so she got in trouble a lot. She found friends on the streets to hang out with.

Baltimore Steps and Billie Dove

Billie cut school one time too many and a probation officer hauled her in to face a judge. The judge could see that no one was really taking care of her, so he sent her to a home for minors without proper care and guardianship called The House of Good Shepherd for Colored Girls. Billie was nine years old. Most of the girls were older than Billie and had committed crimes. Some of them were very tough and bullied her. The nuns were very strict and some of them hit the girls with rulers. Billie never received much affection there. Christine Scott worked in the kitchen at Good Shepherd and remembers Billie as a quiet, neat, good-looking girl. "She was always down in the dumps. She had nothing to do with nobody else." After about a year, her mom Sadie came to take her back home to try and make a new start.

Listening example: *I Cover the Waterfront* **by Billie Holiday**
https://youtu.be/rEJx3dVWCnk

I Cover the Waterfront

Sadie and Billie moved to Fell's Point because it was a neighborhood they could afford. It turned out to be even worse than their former neighborhood. Sadie was often out working and Billie would cut school and go outside and look for fun, excitement and money. She found all three in the "good time houses" nearby. These were houses where men would come and pay money to drink and hang out with good-looking women. Billie was only ten or eleven years old, but she looked older. She would get all dressed up, put on make-up and the men loved her. Sometimes they gave her some money, too. This was a very dangerous life for grown-ups, but even more treacherous for a child.

Many of the good time houses had pianos in them and musicians who came to play for the party people. Some of the houses even had *Victrolas* or *gramophones* (an early type of record player – before CD's) and many of the hot records of the day. Most people couldn't afford to have a Victrola so it was here that Billie first heard Louis Armstrong's singing and trumpet playing. She was completely knocked out by the sound and style of Pops' voice. The first song she heard was *West End Blues.*

Listening selection: *West End Blues* **by Louis Armstrong**

https://youtu.be/zPgh7nxTQT4

She had never heard a voice that was so warm and expressive, like you were his personal friend and he was telling you a secret. When he sang, he *scatted* and bent the notes around like a horn. Louis' singing and playing style deeply inspired Billie. Like Louis, she practiced using her voice to play all around with the rhythm of a song and change the melody to express it in her own way. Billie idolized Louis all of her life. Later in life, they became friends and recorded some wonderful duets together.

Victrola Dreams

It was during this time, also, that Billie first heard the great blues *belter*, Bessie Smith; *The Empress of the Blues.* Bessie had been singing since the days before the microphone was invented: she could belt out a song so loud and clear, that folks 100 feet away and up in the far balconies, could hear every word. Her singing really inspired Billie. Bessie's sound was big and strong, with plenty of attitude, challenge and tease. And Bessie shot straight from the heart. Billie felt the power of strong, honest emotions that blazed from every song.

Listening selection: *Do your Duty* by Bessie Smith

https://youtu.be/G9iKRma6zk4

Billie started singing along with recordings of Louis and Bessie. She learned their music by heart and just kept on singing. She finally found something that was just for her and could make her feel happy. Other people really began to notice her. She was big and beautiful and wow, could she sing!

Good Mornin' Heartache

In 1937 Billie took 2 big hits to her heart when she learned about the tragic loss of two people who meant a lot to her: her father Clarence Holiday and *The Empress of the Blues*, Bessie Smith. Both died in the same year…Bessie (age 41) in a bad car accident and Clarence (age 39) from a lung disorder that he got from exposure to deadly mustard gas, while serving his country in World War I. Bessie and Clarence might have survived except for the racism of those times. While Bessie lay dying by the side of the road, there were delays because the nearby hospital and ambulance only accepted white people. By the time the black ambulance came a long distance to bring patients of color to the hospital that accepted blacks, it was too late to save her. When Billie's father Clarence tried to get treatment for his lung condition, he was turned away from a white hospital and couldn't get to the black hospital in time to save his life. Billie felt these unjustifiable tragedies deeply.

Listening example: *Good Mornin' Heartache* by Billie Holiday

https://youtu.be/-3jO-3BoGzM

Billie was fascinated by the music she heard spilling out of the good time spots. Sadie was away working a lot in New York City. She left Billie in the care of one Miss Lu. Miss Lu tried to control Billie and make her stay home at night and get up for school the next day. But Billie was not about to listen to Miss Lu. Billie was becoming tough and strong. She could stand up to anybody that made her mad. Her good looks and singing talents made her popular. She never wanted to end up like her mother; working her life away, for very little money and no respect. So she found ways to sneak out of the house and follow the sounds of the music.

Listening selection: *Tain't Nobody's Bizness if I Do* by Billie Holiday
https://youtu.be/JAbMlxUhjTs

Sadie was not happy with the news from Miss Lu. She knew her daughter was out of control and decided to send for Billie to join her up in New York City. It was the early 1930's and Billie was about 14 years old. When Billie got to New York City, she got off at the wrong train stop and got lost. Eventually she found her way to Sadie and they discovered the magic of Harlem.

Drop me off in Harlem!

Harlem was an exciting, mostly black neighborhood on the upper west side of
Manhattan Island in New York City filled with elegant old brownstone houses
and leafy trees. Music overflowed from the many music spots. There were clubs,
cafes, dance halls and juke joints where local people and the greatest musicians,
dancers, actors, photographers, writers, artists of color from all over would come,
dressed in the latest styles! People had music parties in their homes and they'd
charge people a little money to come in. These were called *rent parties* because
they helped folks raise money to pay the rent and come together to hear swingin'
music, eat delicious food, dance and party. In the 1930's New York City was
pretty divided along color lines with mostly people of color uptown in Harlem
and mainly white people downtown. But the exciting sounds of jazz and blues
and Latin music were erasing the racial divisions and bringing people together.
White people couldn't resist traveling uptown to Harlem at night to be part of it.
There were so many fantastic musicians, such as Duke Ellington, Coleman
Hawkins, Chick Webb, (it would be impossible to name them all.) Billie started
hanging out wherever the music was, and began to sing as often as she could.
She was singing all the songs of Louis Armstrong and even imitating his horn
riffs!

Trav'lin' all alone

Listening example: *Trav'lin All Alone* **by Billie Holiday:**

https://youtu.be/MBuQm5S84As

Billie walked up and down the Harlem streets looking for work and forced herself to walk into a club that had a piano. Later on in her life, she remembered her first professional singing experience:

"So, I asked him to play *'Trav'lin' All Alone'* that came closer than anything else to the way I felt. And some part of it must have come across. The whole joint quieted down. If someone had dropped a pin, it would have sounded like a bomb. When I finished, everybody in the joint was cryin' in their beer and I picked thirty-eight bucks up off the floor…..when I showed Mom the money for the rent and told her I had a regular job singing for eighteen dollars a week she could hardly believe it!"

"Look, Ma, they paid me for singing!"

Around 1933, Billie was singing in a joint called Monette's Supper Club on 133rd Street in Harlem. It was there that the young music fan and producer John Hammond first heard her. He had often gone up to listen to the owner, Monette, who was a very good singer, but he was blown away by Billie! Hammond recalled hearing Billie for the first time, "She was not a blues singer, but sang popular songs in a manner that made them completely her own. She had an uncanny ear, an excellent memory for lyrics and she sang with an exquisite sense of phrasing....Further, she was absolutely beautiful, with a look and a bearing that was indeed Lady-like, and never deserted her....I decided that night that she was the best jazz singer I had ever heard...."

John Hammond went out night after night to listen to Billie wherever she was singing. He arranged for her to record her first record with some of the best musicians on the scene. One of them was young Benny Goodman with his clarinet who was soon to become very famous. Billie was on her way!

Listening selection: *Mother's Son-in-Law* by Billie Holiday w Benny Goodman

https://youtu.be/XIfyrnzh5Lo

Prez and Lady

Billie had been living in New York since she was a teenager and knew her way around. When she met some bodacious young musicians new to New York City from the Kansas City scene, she took Lester Young the tenor sax player, and the trumpet player Buck Clayton under her wing and showed them all of the hot music spots. They had groovy times going to nightclubs, listening, jamming and having a ball. They called themselves *The Unholy Three*. Billie was 19 and Lester and Buck were in their 20's. There was music every night, all night, all over New York and Harlem was the center of it all. Lester was becoming a music star and Billie loved his playing more than any musician she had ever heard. Around 1934, Lester moved into the Harlem apartment of his friend Billie and her mom, Sadie, and rented a room from them. Plus Sadie's fried chicken was famously delicious.

Lester and Billie were musical soul mates. They had a special friendship and understood and appreciated each other deeply as fellow artists with sensitive feelings and as people. The music they made together is like an intimate conversation between good friends only instead of talking, they speak in the language of music. Billie's voice floats and twists in horn-like tones and Lester plays little musical comments of support, agreement, sympathy….it's all there, if you listen. These were magical sounds that touched peoples' hearts for all time. Both Billie and Lester made many more recordings with hundreds of other artists over the following years but the quality of love and understanding that you hear and feel when Lady sang with Prez stands out as some of the greatest sounds in jazz history.

Listening selection*: A Sailboat in the Moonlight* by Billie Holiday and Lester Young   https://youtu.be/tJxVzhzle2I

Listening selections: *When You're Smiling,* https://youtu.be/LC_XM4l1DHo

Prez and Lady: a Musical Friendship

Billie said, " I always try to sing like a horn--a trumpet or tenor sax, and I think Lester is just the opposite. He likes to play like a voice...Lester sings with his horn. You listen to him and you can almost hear the words." She described Lester Young's music by saying, "(it) flips you out of your seat with surprise! "

Prez and Lady Day made special music together. Here's what some people had to say about it: Writer Whitney Balliett describes the effect of Holiday and Young together at their best as "a single voice split in two."

The great pianist Jimmy Rowles said "The way Lester played behind her, these fill-ins, she would feel like she was just in her mother's arms…she was always happy when she knew Prez was standin' right there, playing for her…because what he did was for her…they were perfectly matched… .At times, she's singing and he's playing, both, like intertwined vines…their music is more than anything, about the pleasure of playing together, of sharing a skill. Think what it must have felt like to be Holiday. Not only can she sing, but she is given the best possible musicians to work with, and the languid guy in slippers is as close to a soul-mate musically, as she'll ever be likely to find. Together they define pleasure in the best possible way, by living it".

Nicknames, Monikers, Handles and Labels

The story goes that Lester gave Billie the nickname that she would use for the rest of her life, "Lady Day". Billie claimed to have given Lester his famous nickname, too: *Prez*. She explained, "The greatest man around in those days was (President) Franklin Delano Roosevelt, so I started calling Lester *The President* (later shortened to *Prez*). He called me *Lady* and my mother was *Duchess*. We were *The Royal Family of Harlem*. Lester called Billie *Lady Day* because she always looked like an elegant lady and he added on, part of her last name; *Holi – day*.

Nicknames, also called monikers, handles or labels, have always been super important for musicians. They deepen the bond between musicians and music lovers. Nicknames can also help to remind musicians that who they are and what they do is truly important, even though racism could destroy the music or the musicians at any moment and sometimes did. Some nicknames are compliments and sound heroic; like titles of royalty such as *Duke Ellington, Count Basie, Nat King Cole, Queen of the Trumpet* (Valaida Snow). Titles of royalty also let folks know that this person deserves respect, which helped to counter - balance the negativity of American racism. Other nicknames highlight the person's talents such as *Hot Lips Page, Cannonball Adderley, Willie The Lion Smith*. Other nicknames are humorous and fun like *Satchmo, Dizzy, Bird, Cootie, Bean, Jelly Roll, Big Eye, Sweets, Bags, Cleanhead, Mr. Five by Five*.

God Bless the Child

Billie's star was really on the rise. She began singing in beautiful dance and concert halls. She was earning more money and got to wear beautiful, elegant clothes. But there were many more storms to come. The racism of the times still made her life a living hell sometimes. Taxi drivers would not pick her up because she was a woman of color. When she went on the road, travelling with some of the most popular bands, such as the Count Basie Band and Artie Shaw, the white musicians were treated decently, while the musicians of color were treated less than human. Black musicians weren't allowed to eat or use the same bathrooms as white people. It was still "Back of the Bus" rules known as *Jim Crow*, with segregated drinking fountains, bathrooms, public places, and people of color had to go around to the rear entrance. When the band arrived at the performance venue, Billie would change into her performance clothes, walk onstage in her elegant gown with white gardenias in her hair and give the audience the best show they ever heard.

Back in Harlem, Billie was now quite a celebrity and earned enough money to help her mom, Sadie, so that she wouldn't have to work so hard. But things weren't always smooth sailing. Sometimes Billie and Sadie didn't see eye to eye and things could get very salty. After one of their quarrels over money, Billie went out and wrote down her feelings. She wrote about how people want you when you have money, but let you down when the money is gone. She wrote "God bless the child that's got his own," which counsels the child inside of us to get what they need for themselves so you don't have to go begging anyone else, even family, for help. Be strong and stand on your own two feet. These words are in the lyrics to her most famous song, *God Bless the Child,* which became a huge hit in 1941. It is still being sung today, in 2017.

Listening selection: *God Bless the Child* by Billie Holiday

https://youtu.be/bKNtP1zOVHw

God Bless the Child

Strange Fruit

Strange Fruit is a powerful and haunting ballad about the horrors of lynching black people. This was a common practice mostly in the Southern states of America. In Billie's lifetime there were plenty of people still around who witnessed human beings strangled by ropes and hung up on trees and left to die. This was called lynching and of course, it wasn't legal. But black people often were convicted and put to death for crimes that would only be a short prison sentence for a white person. Most people that Billie knew had seen things done to blacks simply in the name of racial prejudice that chilled the soul and nearly killed hope. But a song about it? There is probably no other song in all of jazz that carries such a harsh, truthful and moving message. *Strange Fruit* started out as a poem by Abel Meeropol, a Jewish high school teacher from the Bronx, New York. Using the name Lewis Allan, Meeropol composed the music for *Strange Fruit* and gave it to Billie. Once she sang it, it became forever associated with her. At first she wasn't sure how audiences would take such a brutally honest song. But she bravely decided to go for it. Singers in those days mostly did light-hearted happy songs that people could dance to, or dark, dramatic, romantic songs about the pain of lost love. No one sang about the harsh realities of racism and the murder of black people. But Billie took her chances and stood up in nightclubs and concert halls to sing this song. People who heard her sing it were deeply moved.

She usually saved it for last. *Strange Fruit* became her biggest selling record. She must have sung it thousands of times in her career, but even so, it always moved her. Her piano player Bobby Tucker said that Billie always broke down in tears every time she sang it. Singing *Strange Fruit* made Billie more than just a jazz singer. She became a brave person speaking out against injustice. That's what we call *activism* today. No one knew better than Billie how unfairly people of color were treated. Speaking out about it takes courage. It could even be dangerous. People might challenge you or even hurt you. But she had the guts to take her chances and she made it.

Everywhere she went, audiences and musicians loved hearing Billie sing. She had written hit songs and appeared in movies. She travelled all over. Her career was hitting all the high notes. She always had her beloved dogs with her. She had everything except happiness. The men she chose to love were always users or abusers; beaters or cheaters. Billie had been using drugs and alcohol to dim the pain, loneliness, anger and frustration she felt, since she was a young girl in

Baltimore. She was arrested several times and spent time in jail. Each time she got out, she tried to stay straight and healthy. But she never could, for long. By the late 1940's, her health was starting to go downhill. On March 15, 1959, Billie went to the funeral of her dear friend, Prez. She said, "I'll be the next to go."

Strange Fruit

Listening selection: *Strange Fruit* by Billie Holiday

https://youtu.be/c52ElU5tQNo

Laughin' at Life

Many bad things happened to Billie Holiday in her childhood. From her teenage years and throughout her short life, she had problems that led to drug addiction and jail time. She wanted to be loved and cared for so desperately, that she often gave her love and trust to bad people. Some of them robbed her and roughed her up. Newspapers, magazines, books and films mainly focus on Billie's struggles with her terrible problems. Many people think that people who take drugs or drink alcohol are bad people. But the mistakes that Billie made are not the most important or interesting things about her life. In spite of a sad life that can be horrifying to think about, Billie's life is a meditation on keeping true to your own musical expression and bouncing back after the world knocks you down. Each time she got kicked down, she got back up, and came out swingin'! It was during her last, hardest years that she recorded one of her finest recordings, *Lady in Satin* with a lush string orchestra. The beautiful voice is not much more than a rusty rasp yet the way she expresses the story is hard to forget… Lady's artistry only increased with her troubles.

Listening selection: *The End of a Love Affair* **by Billie Holiday**
https://youtu.be/oxSldEPISwo

Laughin' at Life **by Billie Holiday : https://youtu.be/GuXkSMW-8ls**

But in the summer of 1959, Billie became very ill. She died in New York City on July 22, 1959. She was 44 years old. Billie Holiday had many hit records and sang all over the United States and in Europe. She created a style of singing that was different. She approached singing like a great musician plays a horn. She wrote some unforgettable songs. She was brave and took chances that some of the messages in her songs might turn people against her. She spoke out against the way blacks were treated. She was very popular and beautiful and changed jazz singing forever. She freely gave her gift of music to the world. "It is sad beyond words that [Lady Day] never knew how many people loved her…she really was happy only when she sang" (Ralph Gleason).

Back in your own Backyard: **https://youtu.be/ns8Hm77J6Bs**

Listening selection: *I'll be seeing you* **by Billie Holiday**
https://youtu.be/zDlKb2cBAqU

Lady Day's Legacy: There are so many books and articles about Billie Holiday that it is impossible to name them all, so here are some: *Wishing on the Moon; The Life and Times of Billie Holiday* by Donald Clarke, *Billie's Blues; The Billie Holiday Story 1933-1959* by John Chilton, *Lady Sings the Blues:* book by Billie Holiday and William Dufty, *Lady Sings the Blues*: film starring Diana Ross, Billy Dee Williams, Richard Pryor; *Lady Day at Emerson Bar and Grill:* stage play by Lanie Robertson starring many great actress/singers who've played Billie Holiday including

Lonette McKee, S. Epatha Merkerson, and Audra McDonald, *"Lady Day – The Musical"* starring Dee Dee Bridgewater on Broadway, *Lady Day: A Musical Tragedy in 2 acts* by Aishah Rahman, The Billie Holiday Theatre: a theatre named after her in Brooklyn, New York, and many other plays, songs, books, articles, photos, portraits, imitators, emulators and impersonators. She wins new fans every year and her power to inspire us just keeps on growing!

Jazz Glossary

Big ears = Great ability to hear, understand, appreciate music

Cat = male

Chick = female

Dig = appreciate, understand

Drag = event or person that gets everyone down

Fill-ins or fills = to fill in the spaces left by the first player or singer with musical responses

Funky = smelly, dirty but really expresses the spirit of the music

Gig = a music job

Groove, groovy = "in the groove" came from the indentations on old records, and when the needle slipped into the groove, the music happened. *The groove* in jazz, is when all the musician are listening to each other, the music and emotions come together and the band takes off!

Hot = Soulful, daring, emotional and blues-soaked style, usually associated with black musicians

Jamming = a casual music session for sharing musical ideas and explorations

Jim Crow laws = Racial Segregation Laws in the South from the 1860's until overruled by The Civil Rights Act of 1964 and The Voting Rights Act of 1965. These laws included segregated drinking fountains, bathrooms, public spaces, making people of Color sit at the back of buses, etc. For more information: https://en.wikipedia.org/wiki/Jim_Crow_laws

Joint = place where music is played, or just a place

Kitty = female

One-nighters = a band tour that stops in a new location every night (very tiring!)

Monikers, handles, labels = nicknames

Riff = short improvised melodic phrase in music

Scat singing, scatting = a vocal solo using improvised words or sounds, sometimes imitating instruments or animals.

Shedding = practicing, as in "going to the woodshed" (to practice where no one can hear you.

Sitting in = spontaneous participation as a guest performer on someone else's gig.

Sweet = beautiful jazz with polished tone and delivery

Swing = when the music really makes you want to move

Time = rhythm

Torch Song = romantic song expressing heartbreak, loneliness sung in a sensual, dramatic style.

Acknowledgments

This work is dedicated to my brother Stu: the first super hero who saved my life and to my mother Frances, for her stories….love, support, patience, encouragement, and food have come to me in grateful measure from the men I love: my fiancé Louis Colon, and my son Sean-Francis who at age 4, declared with a sigh, *"My mom has a voice like music!"*

Words alone cannot convey my deep gratitude to Dr. Marion Nesbit for the inspiration, nurturance and creative support that she gave so generously, and to my fantastic team at Lesley University: Mili Bermejo-Greenspan and Dominique Eade. Much appreciation goes out to many others including Alison Armstrong, Dr. Susan Barile, Jeanie Black, Stuart Brotman, Stanley Crouch, Dr. Douglas Henry Daniels, Anita Evans, Henry Ferrini, Will Friedwald, Will and Mae Gamble, Pastor John Garcia Gensel, Dan Gaynor, Gary Giddens, Kappi Hansen, Barry Harris, Val Hawk, Gitesha Hernandez, Willie Jones, Sherry Lane, Janet Lawson, Phyllis Lodge "Pal", Herb Lovelle, Jeanette LoVetri, Larry Lucie, Wynton Marsalis, Sarah McLawler, Judy Niemack, Madeline Yayodele Nelson, Iya Nirvana, Lewis Porter, Benny Powell, Phil Schaap, Ed Schuller, Norman Simmons, Billy Smith, Anna Maria Spallina, Laura Vaccaro, Claude "Fiddler"

Williams, The Lester Young, Jr. family, Webster Young, and always and ever, Dennis Irwin.

Artwork: Cover portraits: Phil Blank

Inside illustrations: Masha Somova

Cover Design, additional art: Adrian Doan Kim Carames

Bibiography

Clarke, Donald *Wishing on the Moon; The Life and Times of Billie Holiday.* New York: Viking, 1994, 121

Collier, James Lincoln. *The Great Jazz Artists.* New York: Four Winds Press; Scholastic Magazines, Inc. 1977: 127.

Gleason, Ralph J. *Celebrating the Duke and Louis, Bessie, Billie, Bird, Carmen, Miles, Dizzy, and Other Heroes: And Louis, Bessie, Billie, Bird, Carmen, Miles, Dizzy and Other Heroes.* Da Capo Press, 1995: 75 - 76, 79, 80 - 81

Hammond, John, Townsend, Irving. *John Hammond on Record.* New York: Ridge Press, 1977: 87

Martin, Marvin. *Extraordinary People in Jazz.* New York & Ontario: Scholastic, 2004: 69 – 71.

Missouri Review: www.missourireview.com/content/dynamic/view-text.php?text-id=1936-59K-

Novesky, Amy, Newton, Vanessa Brantley. *Mister and Lady Day: Billie Holiday and the Dog Who Loved Her.* HMH Books for Young Readers, 2017

Swed, John *Billie Holiday The Musician and the Myth* New York: Penguin 2016

44582075R00015

Made in the USA
Middletown, DE
09 May 2019